Towns and Villages
OF ENGLAND

WILTON

To James

With Best Wishes

Chris Rousell

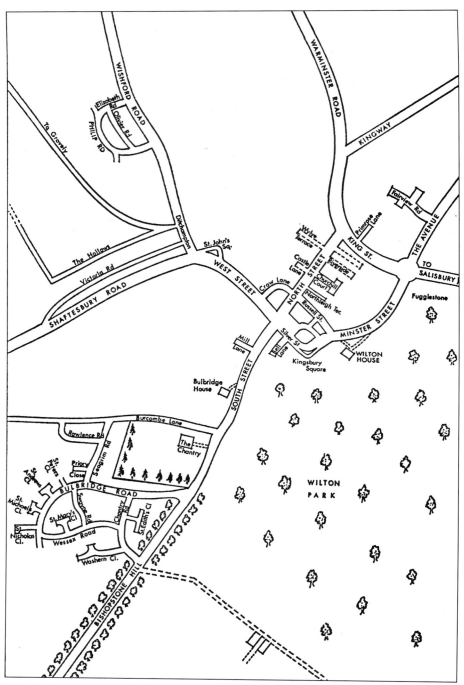

Street plan of Wilton

Towns and Villages OF ENGLAND

WILTON

C H R I S   R O U S E L L

ALAN SUTTON

First published in the United Kingdom in 1993 by
Alan Sutton Publishing Limited
Phoenix Mill · Far Thrupp · Stroud · Gloucestershire

First published in the United States of America in 1993 by
Alan Sutton Publishing Inc · 83 Washington Street · Dover · NH 03820

British Library Cataloguing in Publication Data

Roussell, Chris
  Towns and Villages of England: Wilton
  I. Title
  942.319

  ISBN 0-7509-0464-X

Library of Congress Cataloging in Publication Data applied for

Typeset in 11/13 Bembo.
Typesetting and origination by
Alan Sutton Publishing Limited.
Printed in Great Britain by
Hartnolls Ltd, Bodmin, Cornwall.

Contents

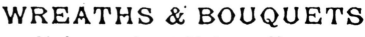

F. W. MARKS,

(Late E. SLOW)

Carriage Builder

 **AND** *Wheelwright,*

West End, WILTON,

WILTS.

CARRIAGES BOUGHT OR SOLD ON COMMISSION.

Repairs Neatly Executed.

PAINTING, REPAIRING,

And every description of work connected with the Trade

Executed on the Premises.

PERSONALLY SUPERINTENDED.

ESTIMATES GIVEN.

CHAPTER ONE

Early History

The first settlers to establish themselves in the area which today is known as Wilton were a small tribe of Anglo-Saxons who had migrated from the south. On reaching here they found ideal conditions which suited their requirements, a fertile valley basin situated between the two rivers of the Nadder and the Wylye, and surrounded by rich agricultural land. The nearby downland was also ideal in forming natural defences.

It was not long after the establishment of the settlement that the Saxons consolidated their power in the area and Wilton became the local royal administrative centre, eventually becoming the royal town of Wessex. Exactly when Wilton became a royal town is not known, but it is thought that a royal palace could have been in existence early in the seventh century. There is evidence of this in records of charters being signed at Wilton in 838 and 854. The latter referred to the ratification of the decisions of King Ethelwulf when he tithed his lands at a council in Winchester, and was signed by the king, giving the location of the signing as the palace at Wilton. Certainly by the early ninth century the king had a palace here, which also served as a place for keeping royal archives and issuing royal charters.

Kingsbury Square is most likely to have been the area in which the palace was situated (Kingsbury meaning the stronghold of the king), and this area is no doubt the historic core of the town. In front of the palace and its grounds was an open market area surrounded by houses and a small minster church, the site of which is now occupied by the ruined church of St Mary's in the market place. It is thought this minster church would have been of some importance in the eighth century and its close association with the royal palace is indicated by the fact that at least two of Edward the Elder's daughters are buried there, along with his second wife.

The defences of the town became a significant feature in the general defence of Wessex, and with Wilton being such an important town during the ninth and tenth centuries, they provoked various attacks by the Danes. In 871 King Alfred fought a fierce battle with them just outside the town on high ground in the area which is now in the grounds of Wilton Park, on the Earl of Pembroke's estate. After their defeat the Danes took revenge and sacked and burnt the town. It was about this time, just after the defeat of the

Borough seal, 1362

Danes, that Alfred was reputed to have refounded the priory dedicated to St Mary, removing it from its present position to the site which had been occupied by the royal palace, and giving this new benefice the title of abbey.

Before the foundation of the abbey, there was already an ecclesiastical presence in Wilton, the first religious establishment as such being recorded in about the year 800. This was when Weohstan, the first recorded Earl of Wiltshire, founded a chantry for secular priests by converting an old church called St Mary's and dedicating it to the memory of Alemund. After Weohstan's death, his wife persuaded King Egbert to convert the chantry into a priory for thirteen nuns and to dedicate it to St Mary, with Weohstan's wife becoming prioress.

The abbey soon became important, not only as a religious centre and giving the abbess a great amount of power, but also for its high reputation for teaching. Many Saxon princesses and daughters of noblemen received their education there. They were taught many subjects, including needlework, confectionery, writing, drawing, surgery and physic. The last two subjects were taught because in those days many religious establishments took in the sick and treated them in hospitals which were attached to the establishments, with monks and nuns performing the treatment.

West Street, showing St John's Priory Almshouses on the right, late 1940s

One cannot, of course, ignore St Edith, Wilton's patron saint, when writing about the abbey. She was the daughter of Wulfrith (who was later to become abbess) and King Edgar, who, as a result of a visit to the abbey in 960, met and became infatuated with her. For making her pregnant, Edgar was made to pay a penance by St Dunstan for his sin of violating the sanctity of the cloister.

Edith was born at Kemsing in Kent, returning to the abbey with her mother to receive her education, and becoming proficient at singing, music, writing, painting, embroidery and sculpture. It was said that she was meek, and full of charity and self-denial. While at the abbey she also built a chapel in the grounds, which she dedicated to St Denis. Tragically, she died of a fever on 16 September 984 at the age of 23, and was buried in the chapel which she had built. Her early death had been foretold by St Dunstan when he consecrated the chapel after its building.

During its first two hundred years the abbey grew and prospered, receiving many benefactions of land. It was also given the right to hold fairs in the town, which did not go down too well with the burgesses. They held fairs of their own, and this led to conflict with the abbey. But the abbey's possessions dwindled during its final 150 years and discipline also suffered. Its rights were also heavily interfered with by Henry VIII and Cardinal Wolsey. On 25 March 1539 the reigning abbess, Cecelia Bodenham, surrendered the abbey and its lands to the king, who in turn granted them to William Herbert, the

Wilton House

eldest son of Sir Richard Herbert, whose family was of welsh origin and prominent in Glamorgan and Monmouth during the latter part of the fifteenth century. While fighting in France, William's courage brought him favour with Francis I who, in turn, recommended him to King Henry VIII.

After his return to England he married Anne Parr, sister to Catherine, sixth wife of Henry VIII. In 1542 he was granted a coat of arms and crest and, two years later, Wilton Abbey and its lands. He immediately set about demolishing the abbey and commenced the building of a house for himself on the site, using stone from the abbey for its construction. The house was completed in 1550, a grand building constructed around a courtyard. In October of the following year William was made Lord Herbert of Cardiff and Earl of Pembroke. Thus began a family line at Wilton that survives to the present day.

In 1552 he entertained Edward I at the house and after the king's death in 1553 continued to find royal favour through the reigns of Mary and Elizabeth, and during this time wielded considerable power at court. He died at Hampton Court in 1570.

The Palladian Bridge, Wilton House

William was succeeded by his eldest son Henry, who made some substantial alterations to the house in the early years of the seventeenth century. The new work possibly involved the advice of the great architect and designer Inigo Jones. It was through his wife Mary Sidney that during this time the house became well-known for its patronage of the arts, and many learned people of the period were regular visitors, including Philip Massenger, Ben Jonson, Samuel Daniel and Edmund Spencer. Mary's brother Sir Philip Sidney spent much time at the house and is reputed to have written *Arcadia* while there, dedicating it to his sister.

Tradition has it that Shakespeare and his company gave the first performance of *As You Like It* before King James I at Wilton House in 1603 and it is also said that the first performance of *Twelfth Night* took place there.

In 1647 there was a disastrous fire which destroyed much of the house. Inigo Jones is again believed to have been involved in the rebuilding but much of the work was probably by his nephew John Webb.

Early in the nineteenth century the eleventh earl employed James Wyatt in a programme of extensive rebuilding and redesign both inside and out. Although the Wilton House we see today is the result of several stages of rebuilding, it is thought likely that the overall shape and much of the masonry of the present Wilton House correspond closely to that of Herbert's original design; the architectural detail has been completely changed.

The entrance gate, Wilton House

During the existence of the abbey it was reported that Wilton had no less than twelve churches, but many of these were not churches in the sense that we might think of them today. Many were only simple meeting or prayer houses, but even so they were still considered churches in the broadest sense.

Sites of some of these ancient churches are known, but the majority are only indicated by an area, and therefore only show the vicinity where a church once stood. One of these churches has already been mentioned, the church of St Mary's, or as it was known in these earlier periods, St Mary's church, Brede Street. (This street was in the market place, where the bus stop is today.) The church remained in use until 1845 and was the parish church of the town, but when it became badly in need of repair it was decided to build a new parish church in West Street.

It was at St Mary's church that Robert Bingham was consecrated as Bishop of Salisbury, at the time when Salisbury Cathedral was being built. During the thirteenth century the church was partly rebuilt, and in the eighteenth it was restored again. Despite all this restoration it still became badly in need of repair and caused great concern during the early part of the nineteenth century. When the new parish church opened, St Mary's was partly demolished, leaving only the nave and chancel remaining in use until the chancel was converted into a small chapel where services took place for a number of years.

View of the ancient parish church of St Mary's, with ivy covering its ruined walls, early 1900s

The interior of the old parish church of St Mary's in the market place, early 1900s

In this area of the market place is the site of another church which was called Holy Trinity. Its exact site is not known today, but it was probably situated opposite the Guildhall. It was a church of the Guild of Merchants and was established in the twelfth century. As a guild church it was used by the

The ruins of St Mary's

burgesses, especially at times of elections. Another church of importance was in South Street and called St Michael's. In 1200 Gospatrick of Wilton was baptised there.

Two more churches were situated in West Street: St Nicholas and another St Mary's. The latter was really more of an ancient rectory, of which the abbess was patron. St Nicholas was reported to be a rectory, and it seems to

Wilton Church

C.J.ROUSELL

The parish church

have been in ruins before 1435. It was on, or very near to, the site of this church that the present parish church was built. When the church was being built, the remains of persons buried in the churchyard of the former church were found on the site. When the new church was completed these bones were reinterred in the sarcophagus on the west wall outside the church.

The new parish church was built between 1841 and 1845 and was a gift of Lord Herbert of Lea, a friend of Florence Nightingale. He was also at this time holding the post of Secretary of War, brought about as a result of the Crimean War.

The church is built in the Northern Lombardic style, the design being inspired by the Lombardic churches of San Pietro and Santa Maria, situated near Viterbo, north of Rome. The orientation of the church is unusual in that it is on a north–south axis. This is alleged to have been the wish of the Dowager Countess of Pembroke, it being the custom in her native Russia. The church was consecrated in October 1845 by Bishop Denison of Salisbury.

There is much to be seen inside the church, most of the early workmanship having been brought in from abroad, along with many tablets

The altar and choir stalls in the parish church

The interior of the parish church

Stained glass in the parish church

and memorials from the old parish church of St Mary's. One of the main features of the church is its stained glass, much of which is of medieval and Continental origin. It was greatly restored on installation. The glass has been described as turning the church into a museum of beauty.

Nonconformist groups have been in existence in Wilton from the latter part of the eighteenth century. In 1761 there were two houses licensed for Quakers, but they did not last very long. It was not until 1883 that the Quakers became more firmly established, when they acquired a meeting place in Russell Street. They later moved to South Street, and finally abandoned the town in 1911. Congregationalists had their chapel in Crow Lane, which is alleged to have been built on the site of an old Presbyterian meeting house. The church was the largest of the nonconformist churches and in 1829 it was reputed to have had 400 members. In 1851 average congregations were 200 in the morning, 100 in the afternoon and 250 in the evening. Sunday school attendances from morning to evening were 110, 80 and 60. After thriving in the nineteenth century, a decline in attendances became evident in the twentieth, and the chapel shared its minister with congregations at Broadchalke and Ebbesborne Wake.

Methodist houses for the Wesleyan Methodists were registered in 1778, 1780 and 1794. In 1829 they had congregations of 150 members, and about

Interior of the Congregational church

two years later a chapel was built in North Street, remaining in use until about 1936. A congregation was established for Primitive Methodists during the 1830s in a house licensed by William Sanger, resulting in a regular establishment of 40 members. In 1851 attendances at all three services of the day were 32, 48 and 60. A new chapel was built in Kingsbury Square in 1880 and the old one closed. Today this building is shared by the Methodists, the United Reformed Church and the Catholics. A Methodist Reform church opened in Kingsbury Square in 1872, but it did not survive for very long and by 1896 was closed.

An interesting document records the complete list of officials that worked in Wilton in 1247. There were four moneyers, two by the name of William,

Another of Wilton's connections with royalty was the establishment of mints in the town, an activity which took place from 959 to 1250. The mints finally closed down in the reign of Henry III. With only some short breaks, the Wilton mints were in operation for longer than any other Wiltshire mints. One break in operations was caused in the year 1003, when Sweyn, King of Denmark, came with his army and sacked and burnt the town. The moneyers fled to Old Sarum, to carry on their work there for a time. All the coins minted in Wilton were made of silver, their size and weight conforming to standards approved by the king. The penalties for making coins of incorrect weight or inferior quality were very severe, and it was an unpardonable offence to make a false declaration of the number of coins made. One of the penalties was that the hand of the moneyer should be severed at the wrist.

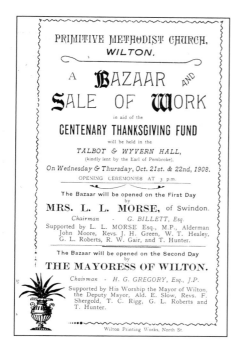

Advertisement for a church bazaar

one called John and the other called Hugh. Two men helped prepare the silver, four assisted in the making of coins, and one kept a record of coins made. It was somewhat unusual for more than one moneyer to be working at the same time in a place the size of Wilton, but it appears that this was in fact the case during the reign of Edward the Confessor, when no less than six moneyers were making coins in the town at the same time.

During the time that Wilton has had borough status, it has received no less than fifteen royal charters. The first was granted by King Henry I in the year 1100, and is thought to be one of the oldest charters in the country. Other charters were granted by various monarchs, the last by Queen Victoria in 1885.

Mayors of the town can be traced back as far as 1256. The mayor was, at that time, a rather dubious character. He was arrested along with one Abraham Russell, a leading Jew in the Jewish community that was established in the town. Wilton was one of twenty-seven centres which held chests on behalf of the Jews for the registration of debts that were owed to them. Russell and the mayor, one William Isembard, were removed from the keepership of the chest for fraudulent practices. Russell managed to escape, but the mayor stood trial, and on being found guilty was hanged in London.

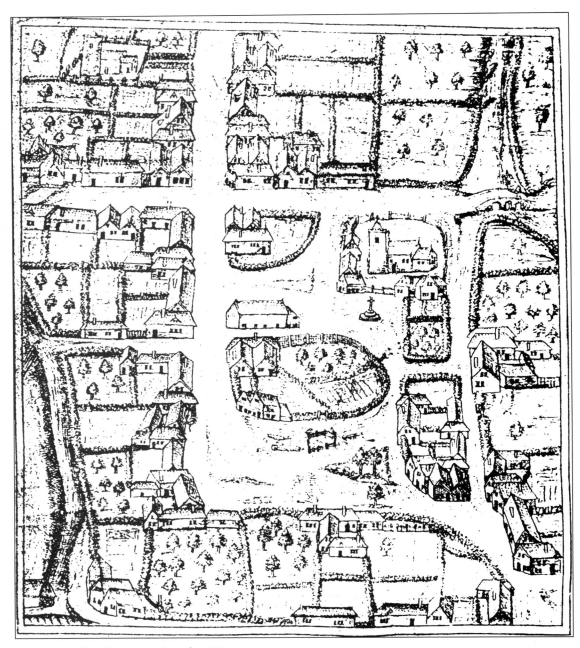

Wilton from a drawing of *c.* 1568

The Mayor of Wilton's seal, 1430

Another mayor, Robert de Brudecombe, who was in office from 1282 to 1299 and again in 1311, had written between his terms what is generally known as 'The Mayor of Wilton's Common Place Book'. This was written on fine vellum in several fourteenth-century hands, and its size was only 8 in by 6 in. Except for just four lines of early English verse, the remainder was written in Latin or Norman-French, examples of the languages necessary to be known at the time by an educated person. It was translated in a type of Chaucerian English with a Wiltshire accent, as used by the 'man in the street'.

This book contained many useful items which were considered to be of some importance in those days, and included matters and circumstances profitable and harmful to most organs of the body. It also had various prayers and meditations, lists of lucky and unlucky days, copies of documents concerning the affairs of the Corporation of Wilton, and various remedies and prescriptions, from a cure for fevers to the assurance of success in love.

Just over one hundred years ago the book was split into two parts. In 1923 one part was found in the Wilton archives and it was not until 1959 that the second portion was found in a tin box in the loft of a house in West Street, and placed in the borough archives. However, the first portion was lost when it was being translated, and so far it has not been found. The second portion has been translated, and during this process it was discovered that some pages were missing.

The long list of Wilton's mayors can be divided into three sections. The first section, up to 1885, is known as the old corporation. The reason for this is that when a new charter was granted in that year, one of the conditions was that a new corporation had to be elected. This new body remained in office until the local government reorganization of 1974, when Wilton lost its borough status and handed over its affairs to the new Salisbury District Council. However, Wilton still retained a town council to look after its interests, and because of its ancient and historic past it was still able to retain its mayor and continue the history that it is proud of.

CHAPTER TWO

Trade and Industry

Up until the end of the thirteenth century the town had great economic importance in the area, at one period retaining a strong Jewish community that was attracted to its industrial and economic pursuits involving a wide variety of crafts.

These craft industries included glovemakers, goldsmiths, tanners and needleworkers. Evidence also suggests that the town had a group of linen workers. Glovers and needleworkers seem to have been in great abundance, each having their own quarter of the town, borne out in the street names Glover Street, Nedlers Street and Nedlers Bridge. All of these have long since disappeared, and all trace of their locations has been eradicated. Complementing the glovers were the tanners. In the last part of the thirteenth century there were at least five of them working in the town.

Markets and fairs attracted a great deal of trade, with merchants bringing in such items as fish, meat, cloth and many other forms of merchandise. Skins, iron, grain and oxen were also traded, and on many occasions, purchases were made at Wilton market on behalf of the king by appointed royal purveyors, because of the presence of royalty in the area.

Many of the traders came to the market from settlements near by, including New Salisbury, which was developing fast. Unfortunately it was eventually destined to take away most of Wilton's trade when Bishop Bingham had a bridge built at Harnham in 1244, giving direct access to New Salisbury and enabling merchants to bypass Wilton. Besides local traders, the market attracted traders from further afield and it was not uncommon for them to travel there from such places as Winchester, Dorchester, Sherborne and Bristol. On the other side of the coin, many traders from Wilton visited markets in other towns to sell their wares, and some of them even specialized in certain items, such as ironmongery.

Brewing was another important activity, especially as the town was a local centre for the distributive trade in wine. Brewing took place in many houses and the operation was undertaken by all classes of society producing and selling ale and cider, many of them women. Tight controls were required and by the middle of the fifteenth century the mayor and burgesses decided to

Market Cross, late 1940s

limit the days on which brewers could actually brew. Only common brewers of the town were allowed to brew without a licence from the mayor, a service for which they had to pay twenty shillings to the common box fund.

Bakers were in great abundance, both in Wilton and its neighbourhood, with fourteen such establishments in operation at the end of the thirteenth century. This trade was governed by very strict regulations and all fourteen bakers had at one time been fined for not strictly obeying them, one or two even committing offences for second and third times, the fines being heavier for each subsequent offence. Other tradesmen, such as butchers and fishmongers, were also subject to very strict regulations.

Decline set in at Wilton between the thirteenth and fifteenth centuries. Once a flourishing town, it eventually lost all its former importance and entered a phase of decay. The decline started when the new bridge was built at Harnham, which in turn led to the rapid growth of New Salisbury. Although Wilton was granted exclusive rights to hold three markets a week, with a three-mile exclusion zone (which included Salisbury) in operation on the days that they were open, the rules were soon disobeyed. Salisbury had been granted a market on one day a week, but it was not long before it was holding markets on the same days as Wilton. This led to a feud between the town and the city; over the ensuing years Wilton was left without any markets at all. Salisbury had taken over.

18

By the middle of the fifteenth century the situation was so bad that Wilton's churches were falling into decay, its bridges in a bad state of repair and many of its tenement houses decaying, with no-one occupying them. Guild rents were also falling and becoming vacant. During the period from 1410 to 1429, the rent for eight shops under the Guildhall fell from 9s. a year to a final permanent price of 7s., and the rent paid by market stalls of 4s. a year was finally reduced to 2s. a year. With such a lack of trade these stalls were abandoned. Attempts were made to revive Wilton's fortunes in 1414 by the granting of a fair which was extended to the following year, but even these efforts failed to stimulate any prosperity. It has often been said that the decline in Wilton's prosperity was due to the dissolution of the abbey, but this does not appear to be the case, as by then almost three hundred years of decline and decay had already taken place.

With practically all the former crafts and trades having virtually disappeared, the only one that seemed to survive to any degree was the textile industry, becoming more important during the sixteenth century than it had ever been in the past. It seems that families of clothiers were the mainstay of the town's commerce at that time, and growing in number. But even their livelihood became threatened to a certain degree when a local mill which took their cloth to be fulled was pulled down in 1545. Fortunately, back in 1536 a Wilton clothier had made arrangements with the abbess of Wilton to lease a mill at Quidhampton, and the loss of the other mill meant that this was now the only fulling-place in operation for Wilton's clothiers, who made full use of its services.

Both narrowcloth and broadcloth were made. Although in the sixteenth century the development of the broadcloth industry was taking place in New Salisbury, merchants were also marketing Wilton cloth as well as their own, much of which was exported overseas. But by the end of the seventeenth century mostly broadcloth was being made. Early in the eighteenth century Wilton was able to start to climb out of decline thanks to the birth of the carpet industry, which had begun to develop from the craft of cloth-weaving.

The first large carpet factory was situated on the site of the Health Centre in the market place. The factory was well established by 1700, but there was also another smaller carpet factory in Kingsbury Square near the post office at this time.

Between 1720 and 1730, this larger factory (which was owned by Moody and Barford) was to receive the services of two French master weavers who were specialists in the making of hand-knotted carpets. Their services for the Wilton factory were obtained by the 8th Earl of Pembroke, who on a visit to France made a tour of their carpet factory at Savonnerie. After inspecting their products he came to the opinion that French and Belgian carpets were

A handmade carpet copied from a painting by Dame Laura Knight, 1930s

far superior to any of those being produced in this country. Wanting nothing but the best for Wilton, he made representations to the French authorities for the 'loan' of two weavers, but permission was refused. However, the earl was not put off so easily. He purchased several large barrels in which to bring home wine, allegedly leaving two of them empty for smuggling the two weavers into this country. On arrival they came to the Wilton factory to teach the weavers their craft, and by 1742 the earl's action had reaped rewards. What became known as 'Wilton Cut Pile Carpet' was to become famous all over the world.

Changes in ownership took place, until eventually the Blackmore brothers, who owned the smaller Kingsbury Square factory, took over the larger one.

Carpet factory designing room, early 1930s

By this time it had become known as the Great Carpet Factory. The former premises of the brothers were used as a store and workrooms. This took place in 1817, but two years later competition greatly increased when the war between England and France ended. A depression took place in the industry and reduced the scale of work. In order to keep them in employment, weavers were given work on the Wilton Estate, building walls, roads and bridges. The wall which runs from Fugglestone to Netherhampton took three years to complete, using a workforce of seventeen men. Although they were only weavers by trade, they made such a good job of it that the wall is still standing today.

The year 1834 saw the closure of the carpet factory in the market place, as well as the factory in Kingsbury Square. Both businesses were transferred to a larger site in King Street occupied by the redundant Burdensball Mill, owned by the Wilton Estate. Records show that there had been a mill on this site since Tudor times, and that it originally started life as a corn and grist mill. In the early part of 1835 the new factory was in production and the owners were in the fortunate position of being able to purchase some looms from the carpet factory at Axminster in Devon, which had gone bankrupt. This sale also gave employment to some of the redundant weavers, a gesture for which they were grateful.

Business grew, and the factory prospered. At certain times during this early period there were nearly 500 men and women employed there, but by the last

Winding the yarn onto the bobbins, prior to being used on the looms

decade of the century the workforce had been drastically reduced to 168, one of the main causes being a shortage of child labour. It is interesting to note that back in the 1700s the local press had published a warning to all mill overseers that they should not apprentice children in or around Wilton. The reason was that many had received cruel treatment, and there had been a death in one instance as a direct result of this cruelty.

Throughout its history the factory experienced many changes in ownership and many ups and downs in its fortunes. In 1903, for example, the company made no profit at all. To try to ease the situation some workers were stood off and others put on short-time working, but despite these last-ditch efforts, the following year the company went bankrupt. The 15th Earl of Pembroke tried without success to interest two London companies in purchasing the factory, so as a last resort the Earl himself saved it for just over £8,000, and successfully formed a company to run it.

It was at about this period that subsidiary factories were opened in Fordingbridge, Downton, Mere and Tisbury, but by 1942 the first three had closed down. The Tisbury factory continued in production until its closure in 1949.

An order was placed in 1905 by King Edward VII for carpeting five rooms in Buckingham Palace, the earl having used his position as Lord Steward to secure the order. The largest carpet for the Bow Reception Room measured just over 60 ft in width and 50 ft in length, its pile being 1 in thick. The carpet had a weight of one ton and it took four months to complete, fifteen weavers being employed in its making. Two of the remaining carpets were made in the actual Wilton weave. The king granted a royal warrant to the factory and shortly afterwards it became known as the Wilton Royal Carpet Factory.

Besides receiving orders from royalty, many other well-known establishments and individuals have used Wilton weavers' skills for carpets

Warminster Road, showing the carpet factory buildings on the left, late 1920s

Hand weaving Wilton carpets, 1940s

handmade to their own requirements. Perhaps the most unusual order was placed by Dame Laura Knight during the 1930s. She asked the factory to make two carpets on which the designs were to be copies of her paintings, one of Pirou and Columbine, the other of Neptune surrounded by water nymphs and sea creatures. Always ready to meet a challenge, the factory's design team managed to resolve the many problems that the order presented, the main one being the difficulty in obtaining the correct scale to reproduce the paintings on carpets that measured 24 ft by 24 ft. The end result was that the whole project was a success. Faithful reproductions were made on each carpet as near to the originals as possible. Notes regarding the Pirou and Columbine carpet show that 2.5 knots were made to the square inch, and a total of 124 colours were used.

The other main industry in the town was felt-making, which was carried on in the mill in Crow Lane. This was originally a grist and malt mill, and used on occasion for fulling cloth for local weavers. In the late 1600s it was purchased by the Earl of Pembroke, who leased it to William Whitchurch in the early part of the next century. Whitchurch proceeded to convert the mill's use to textiles, but between then and 1817 the lease changed hands a number of times. This particular year saw the lease taken over by a partnership who owned a mill in West Street. Besides manufacturing gloves, the mills also made

The courtyard of the carpet factory in the early 1920s

Photograph of a painting by Dame Laura Knight copied for a carpet design, 1930s

a cheap form of carpeting known as 'drugget'. Both establishments remained under its control until a slump in the industry forced the sale of the West Street mill to Lord Pembroke (this mill was later converted into a school); the lease on the Crow Lane mill was eventually taken over by John Brasher.

Up until the end of 1830 the mill did well, but then a group of Swing Rioters attacked the mill, smashing up all the machinery. The men were disgruntled agricultural workers from Wiltshire and the southern counties who had found that farm machinery was taking away their jobs. Low pay and new textile machinery, which took employment away from their wives who used to weave cloth in their own homes, were other problems. As a result of the riots that followed, fifty-five men, women and children were out of employment due to the destruction of machinery. Nine men from Wilton who took part were committed to Fisherton Gaol in Salisbury.

After the riots Brasher continued in the textile trade, but on a much reduced capacity, until 1835 when the lease was taken over by John Naish. A Wilton man, he had owned a mill at Quidhampton which had made Bedford cord until the rioters had practically smashed it beyond repair and reduced its capacity for manufacturing. In 1859 Naish was approached by James Goddard, who suggested that together they should manufacture felt for the pianoforte. Realizing that this product could be a valuable asset to the mill, they made real efforts to market their product both in this country and abroad. Each piano manufacturer required different qualities, and this

General view of West Street in the early 1900s

eventually led to the manufacture of felt taking over operations and Bedford cord being phased out. The range of felt products was widened to include felts for polishing, washers, window channelling, drumstick heads and a wide range of technical felts. Early in the 1900s the manufacture of surgical felts also began. One strange fact, however, is that despite being in a town which manufactures carpets, the mill has never made underfelt.

Young boys were part of the workforce, and there was often some larking about, which on one particular day in the absence of the foreman resulted in tragic circumstances. It appears that one Samuel Leybourne became caught in a belt on the machinery, causing him to be carried upwards and jamming his leg between the belt drum and rafters. In order to free him part of the rafter had to be cut away. His leg was so badly shattered it had to be amputated, but unfortunately Samuel did not survive the experience and died eight days later.

Complaints were made to Wilton Estate that the mill was not up to standard, so in 1880 a tall octagonal chimney was built. The installation of a coal-fired steam boiler helped to bring greater efficiency, by driving a steam engine and a generator to supply electricity. The chimney, which became a feature of the skyline in the town, was demolished in 1959 when a modern oil-fired boiler was brought into use and electricity supplied from the mains. The traditional, heavy type of textile machinery which had been in use for many years serving the mill well was, however, still kept in operation, enabling traditional methods of manufacture to continue.

It was as a result of cloth-weaving and felt-making that Wilton was able to climb out of decline. Rebuilding took place, but despite some changes to the layout of the streets in the central area of the town, many remain virtually the same as in medieval times. The town has long since grown outside its original boundaries; for instance, the little priory church of St John used to be in the parish of Ditchampton, and prior to its building, between 1189 and 1193, the defences of the early settlers were situated in this area of St John's Square. The Royal Forest of Grovely, in which kings often hunted, also extended right down to this part of the town.

CHAPTER THREE

1850–99

According to a street directory of 1851, Wilton seems to have been a thriving community. Its two main industries were providing much-needed employment and there were plenty of shops supplying a wide range of goods for workers and their families to spend money on. Milliners, tailors, grocers, bakers, drapers, dressmakers and a chemist were in evidence, along with a saddler, a harnessmaker and a blacksmith. For those who might require legal advice, there were four firms of solicitors to choose from. All these services were, of course, very much in demand. A visit to Salisbury would entail a long walk there and back for the working classes, so such trips would have been rare.

Despite the air of prosperity that this picture paints, Wilton did have its fair share of poor, who had to rely on regular payments from the poor relief fund. It was helped by Wilton charities, set up through many generous benefactors who were concerned for the welfare of the poor in the town. Two main benefactors were Robert Sumption and Thomas Mease, who between them provided relief from the cradle to the grave. They started by giving maternity benefit to poor married women. After the birth of the child they were provided with baby clothes to the value of £1 5s. by a shopkeeper in the town. When a child could walk and speak, they provided for it to be educated and clothed, and when boys left school provision was made for them to be apprenticed.

For poor young resident women marriage portions were provided, and for the elderly (consisting of five poor men and five poor women, who were natives of Wilton over the age of fifty), a form of old-age pension was provided. In later years the age limit was raised to sixty. At the same time it was agreed that recipients of this charity should also receive additional relief during sickness or other emergencies.

Education of the poor was considered to be important and one of the most famous and well-known establishments for the education of the poor was the Wilton Free School in North Street. It was founded by Walter Dyer of Chancery Lane, London, who in his will dated 19 July 1706 left the sum of £600 to the rector and churchwardens at Wilton on trust, to be used to establish a school in the town for twenty poor boys of the parish. Dyer

Pupils of the Free School in North Street. The photograph was probably taken during the celebration of the school's 200th anniversary in 1914

instructed that the boys were to be taught to read and write, and to be grounded in the rules of common arithmetic, as well as being instructed in the principles and doctrines of the Church of England.

The school opened in 1714 and was run by a board of governors which consisted of the mayor, alderman and burgesses of the borough, working in close harmony with the rector and churchwardens. The charity provided for a schoolmaster at a salary of £20 per year, a rent-free house, and an allowance of £4 a year for the purchase of school stationery and for the heating of the schoolroom during winter months. A further £20 a year was set aside for placing four boys at £5 each into handicraft trades or husbandry. A uniform was provided for the boys, and £25 a year allowed for them to have new uniforms every year at Easter. This uniform, although it was smart, was rather on the quaint side, consisting of a cut-away coat made in a fine buff cloth faced with hyacinth blue, long trousers and buff-coloured caps with black peaks.

Other benefactors contributed to the school and at one point it purchased Redhouse Farm at East Knoyle, which was then let to a tenant farmer, the rent being used to supplement the running of the school. At a later period fee-paying pupils were admitted, as well as boarders who came from Wiltshire, Hampshire and Dorset. There is a record of at least one boarder coming from Newcastle.

The Congregational church in Crow Lane, the adjoining building to the church being the schoolroom and vestry

There were other schools in the town for poor children, some of which started up mainly as Sunday schools. One was attached to the parish church, with forty boys and twenty-five girls attending, plus another twenty-seven children who went to learn to read and write. Nonconformist children had the choice of either the Congregational or Methodist Sunday schools, but by 1835 the latter had closed. The Congregational school, with 156 children, and the parochial school, with 100 children, were still going strong at this time.

At about this period there were also five fee-paying schools, having between them 87 children, and two boarding schools with 18 children.

In 1842 the parochial school became a day school, uniting with the National Society in 1902. It was situated in West Street, the premises having formerly been a cloth mill. They provided accommodation for 310 children, and the teachers' salaries were paid with half of a Board of Education grant. Figures for 1858 reveal that 70 to 80 boys were taught, with 180 to 190 infants being taught by an assistant mistress. It was not until later in the century that girls were admitted.

The Congregational school also converted to a day school and became affiliated to the Union of British Schools. In 1858 it was teaching between 150 and 170 pupils, who were being taught to very high standards. This is verified by the praise given to the school for its teaching and equipment. In 1871 it was still in existence, but it closed later in the century.

West Street with the National School on the right, 1930s

Education for girls was provided by Mrs Sidney Herbert's Church of England School for Girls, situated in a baroque pavilion which had been converted for the purpose in the grounds of Wilton Park. Because of its location it became better known as Wilton Park School. In 1858 it taught between 30 and 40 girls. The main craft was needlework, at which the pupils became specialists. One of their special duties was marking and making Wilton House linen, and after leaving school the girls were in great demand as under-nurses and sewing maids.

In mid-September 1854 cholera broke out in Wilton, which caused great alarm, especially in parishes around the town. The parish of Wilton supplied a very generous subscription to build a temporary hospital on a site adjoining the garden of the workhouse. Fortunately the outbreak was arrested by February the following year, and the hospital was not used again.

A proposal was made in 1854 to light the town with gas, and land was purchased just outside the borough at the back of the workhouse garden by the Wilton Gas Company. Although gas was available to private houses near the carpet factory and the Warminster Road, there was no public lighting. In 1887 the town council made proposals to purchase all the assets of the gas company and after a loan had been secured, the Wilton Gas Order of 1888 was evoked. The corporation was authorized to make the purchase and supply gas to the parishes of Wilton, Burcombe, Fugglestone St Peter and South Newton. This arrangement continued until 1935, when the gas works was closed and all the gas in the district was supplied from Salisbury.

Wilton Park School

The railway arrived at Wilton in June 1856 with the opening of the Great Western Railway (GWR) station in the Warminster Road. The line through Wilton ran between Salisbury and Bristol, joining the main Paddington to Bristol line at Bathampton. It was originally planned to run the line to Chippenham, but influential businessmen intervened. They persuaded the railway company that it would be more beneficial for a direct link to be forged with Bristol, as this would be better for trade.

With the arrival of the railway, new horizons opened up for the town; residents were able to travel further afield much more easily than in the past and in greater comfort, and the transportation of goods to and from the town was of great benefit. There was also the possibility that many more visitors might be encouraged, to boost trade.

Three years later in May another railway station opened in the town, when the Salisbury and Yeovil Railway Company completed its line between Salisbury and Gillingham, which was eventually to link up with Exeter in conjunction with the London & South Western Railway (LSWR). This eventually took over all of the line in January 1878. A new station was built quite near to the GWR one, but it was a little nearer to the town. With two stations in operation, Wilton residents had even more destinations within easy reach of their doorsteps.

To build the line through Wilton the Salisbury and Yeovil engineers had to curve the line sharply just after the avenue bridge, and approximately $4\frac{1}{2}$ acres

Wilton London & South Western Railway station in the early 1900s

of the adjacent sheep fair field were needed to do this. When the owners took advantage of an opportunity to purchase a field next to them, lower down, the railway installed sidings and a loading platform for the sheep fair field. This meant that on fair days thousands of sheep could be brought in by rail, saving many farmers a long and laborious trek by road.

Sheep fairs have been an institution in Wilton for hundreds of years, but the present site only came into use in 1775. In 1883 it was recorded that 40,000 sheep had passed through the fairs in that year and at the September fair in 1901 it was estimated that between 90,000 and 100,000 sheep were penned. The main sheep fairs are held on the second Thursday of August, September and October, and sometimes what is known as a clearance fair is held in November. Since the closure of the railway station all the sheep are brought in by road, but despite the changes that have taken place over the years the traditional practice of penning the sheep in wattle hurdles only ceased in more recent times.

On arrival in Wilton in 1860, one Albert Brewer took up employment as a blacksmith and machinist at the felt mills, but not long after his arrival he established his own business as a blacksmith in West Street, living in a house across the road opposite the forge. The men who worked for him found that he was a hard taskmaster, and being a stickler for punctuality it is alleged that he had a mirror placed on the wall of his bedroom to watch the arrival of the workforce, making a note of all those who arrived late.

Looking towards West Street and showing the former gatehouse (now demolished) next to the Priory Almshouses

Because his workmanship was of such a high standard, his reputation as a blacksmith spread and farmers in the district started to bring him machinery to mend, even asking him to make specific items. Luckily he had an inventive mind and was soon creating special tools to meet the needs of the farmers.

In 1902 the company was sold and the new owner made great changes. Horseshoeing was gradually reduced, but the forges still continued to make harrows, drags etc. The main part of the business was devoted to making and selling agricultural machinery and materials specifically for the farming community, but even though its ownership had changed, the company did not lack inventiveness. It continued to help local farmers with all individual needs and requirements.

Life for the residents in those days was not always serious, and the bank holiday Foresters' fête on 4 August 1873 attracted the largest crowd ever to Wilton Park. The main draw was the French tightrope walker, Blondin, who had achieved fame by successfully crossing the Niagara Falls. On this particular day in Wilton he attracted between twenty and twenty-five

The former Talbot & Wyvern Hall in Kingsbury Square, opened originally as a temperance hall

thousand people from the district, each one paying 1s. admission and getting their money's worth with the performance that he gave. His tricks on a rope suspended 60 ft in the air were certainly amazing, and at one stage, with the aid of special apparatus arranged both above and below the rope, he managed to cook eggs and meat on a special stove, keeping the flames going with a pair of bellows. When he completed the cooking he lowered the food on a rope for some of the crowd to eat. Everyone thoroughly enjoyed his performance, although a few, it is said, thought it too hazardous and sensational!

On the same day at 12 noon, the foundation stone for the new Temperance Hall was laid by Sir Edmund Antrobus, MP for Wilton. The Temperance Society had been formed in the town in 1858, leasing a hall in which to hold their meetings, but this proved to be rather expensive and eventually got the society into debt. Lord Pembroke was sympathetic to the cause and allowed members to hold a demonstration in Wilton Park. Thanks to the success of the event the debt was cleared and sufficient funds remained to purchase land to build a hall.

The object of this new building was to provide a large room for public meetings, open to all without distinction of sect or party. Also to be included in the building were a coffee room, a reading room and a room for what were described as 'innocent games'. In one sense the building was to be a public house without the evil drink. At the time of the laying of the foundation stone, one-sixth of the town's population was teetotal. The building was to be in Doric style and situated in Silver Street, where it meets Kingsbury Square. It was eventually named the Talbot & Wyvern Hall, but to many residents it became more affectionately known as the 'Coffee Tavern'.

Sir Edmund Antrobus retired as MP for Wilton in January 1877. He had represented the town for twenty years. In February, the Hon. Sidney Herbert (later to become the 14th Earl of Pembroke) was elected the town's Conservative MP with 751 votes, gaining a large majority over his opponent, J.S. Norris, who secured only 187 votes. Up until 1832 Wilton had always returned two members to Parliament, but some anomalies were brought to the attention of the parliamentary surveyors in 1832 and the practices were found to be in need of correction. From this date Wilton became a one-member constituency.

On 9 September 1885 there were great rejoicings in the town to celebrate the granting of a new charter. It had incorporated into it extensions to the borough, bringing inside the municipal boundary parts of the parishes of South Newton, Burcombe and Fugglestone St Peter. Their affairs were to be administered by a new corporation, to be elected in November. When the election took place, twenty-one candidates offered themselves for the twelve vacant seats, including a mayor and four aldermen.

Residents were awoken at 4 a.m. when some young men paraded round the town playing a pipe and drum, and two hours later everyone was out and about busily decorating their houses, prior to the grand procession which was to take place through the town later in the day. This was led by a band, immediately followed by men carrying a large banner on which was displayed the names of all the kings who had presented previous charters to the town. Clubs, various organizations and schoolchildren also marched, all displaying banners, with the Foresters in particular making a grand sight in green Robin Hood outfits, and including in their ranks Little John, Will Scarlet and Friar Tuck.

After the procession a free lunch was given in a large tent near the town hall, where five hundred people tucked into large joints of beef, piles of bread and barrels of ale and stout. Later in the afternoon there were various forms

Wilton borough seal, *c.* 1880–1973

of entertainment, from Punch and Judy for the children to a tug-of-war across the river between the Oddfellows and the Foresters, the Oddfellows being the victors when they pulled their opponents into the river. As darkness fell the whole town was illuminated, fireworks were let off and balloons released into the air, after which the band struck up and people danced the night away in the streets. Two years later Wiltonians were dancing once again when Queen Victoria celebrated her Golden Jubilee.

To commemorate this jubilee, a clocktower was erected on the roof of the town hall. The unveiling ceremony was carried out by Lord Pembroke, who said that the Wilton people would certainly know what o'clock it was in future, and 'with that shining monster before their eyes, they would have no excuse whatever if they got behind time, or even too much in front of it'. The clock is older than the tower. Originally intended for the church, it was decided that it would be better placed on the roof of the town hall, as it was a more central site. The clocktower was donated by a retired mayor of the town, Mr W.V. Moore.

The town hall stood on the site of the former Guildhall and was used by the council for its meetings. Although the date 1738 is carved on one of the window-sills, it is widely thought that this refers to the date of its rebuilding. Cells were also provided to hold those persons who fell foul of the law, and

The town hall

the area behind the double doors on the left, as you look at the front of the building, used to be the town's fire station.

On 9 October 1895 the parish church celebrated its jubilee with a service attended by the mayor and corporation, after which a public luncheon took place at the Talbot & Wyvern Hall, presided over by Viscount Folkestone MP. This was followed by a promenade in Wilton Park, the day's celebrations being completed by a full choral service in the church.

The nineteenth century seems to have been one of celebrations for Wiltonians. On a scorching hot day in June 1897 they were once again in celebratory mood, the occasion this time being Queen Victoria's Diamond Jubilee. It was marked with a banquet in the market place for residents of the town, and in the afternoon children had their own festivities, including a free tea. The day was rounded off with a torchlight procession to Grovely Down, where celebrations were completed with the lighting of a huge bonfire.

November 1899 saw Lord Pembroke elected mayor; it was thought that he would be the ideal person to preside at a special celebration the following year which would launch the town into the next century in fine style.

CHAPTER FOUR

1900-38

The highlight of this first year of the new century was the 800th anniversary celebration for the granting of the town's first charter by King Henry I. Many visitors from Salisbury and district also attended the day's events, which commenced with a choral service in the parish church attended by the mayor and corporation. After the service there was a procession to the main gates of Wilton House, led by the volunteer band followed by the mayor and corporation and organizations of the town, which included the Weavers Guild, the Wilton Friendly Society, the Oddfellows and the Foresters, carrying their banners high in the air. All male inhabitants over the age of seventeen were given a free dinner and the children and ladies were given a free tea. To round off the celebrations a firework display was given by Lord Pembroke at his own expense, and this was followed by the usual torchlight procession.

It was not only on special occasions that Wiltonians relaxed. There was an abundance of clubs and societies catering for a wide range of interests, including a Literary Institute, which had a large library of good books, a Constitutional Association, a Liberal Club, a Co-operative Society, Temperance and Total Abstinence Societies and an Association for Gardeners. Young people were catered for with special societies run by both the Congregational and Primitive Methodist Churches, and for those who were sport minded there were cricket and football clubs. If you were artistic there was even an art school.

In the late summer of 1906 there were industrial problems with the staff at the GWR station and because the company made no attempt to resolve them, the station master eventually resigned. It appears that the men who were working there were not pulling their weight. This was making extra work for the station master, and preventing him from going about his normal duties, which he believed was causing the company a loss in revenue. In his letter of resignation he cited the position of his counterpart at the LSWR station, who had more staff at his disposal to start with. They were good workers and this enabled him to get out into the town to meet traders with a view to business. Because of his own situation the GWR station master was unable to do the same, and another complaint was that when he did get sent

North Street, with White's grocery stores on the left (later to become the International Stores), early 1900s

good workers by the company, it was not long before they were removed to work elsewhere. Unfortunately his complaints fell on deaf ears and the resignation was accepted, despite the fact that he had given over forty years of faithful service to the company.

In keeping with its past associations with royalty, the town received a royal visit by King Edward VII and Queen Alexandra on the weekend of 27 June 1908, when they made a private visit to the Earl and Countess of Pembroke at Wilton House. The royal party arrived at Salisbury station and drove from there to Wilton in an open carriage, with thousands lining the route. On arrival at Wilton they were greeted by the mayor, who, with Wilton inhabitants and children cheering loudly, presented the king with the Civic Address. The border and lettering of the address were in beautiful colours, seventeenth-century style. There were also two sepia miniature drawings of Wilton House and the town hall, plus the ancient arms of the borough.

The following day being a Sunday, the royal party attended the morning service at the parish church, driving through streets once again lined with cheering people. In the evening a visit was made to Longford Castle and the following day they returned to London by royal train from the LSWR station at Wilton.

During the departure at the station there was a touching moment concerning the blind daughter of the station master. As the queen walked past the nine-year-old girl, the Countess of Pembroke (who always had a keen

The King and Queen's Visit to Wilton
(Jukes, Wilton)

A crowd awaits the arrival of King Edward VII, June 1908

interest in people's welfare), asked the station master's wife to bring her daughter forward, and then commenced to inform the queen how the girl had only been inflicted with her blindness since March of that year and that it had been diagnosed as incurable. The queen then took the girl's hand, kissed her and said, 'My poor dear child, God Bless You' after which her majesty turned to the daughter of Lady Beatrix Wilkinson who was standing nearby and, joining the two children's hands, said to the other child, 'Take care of this poor little girl', after which she spoke a few words of sympathy to the station master's wife.

The Christmas of 1910 was a miserable one for inhabitants of the Waterditchampton area of the town, due to serious flooding which affected an area from the railway bridge, past the Bell Inn and almost to the church in West Street. The flooding had been due to heavy rain which had caused a torrent of water to rush in from the downs, lying in the area for several days. The depth of the water was sufficient to support a boat. Thirty-four houses were affected, the low-lying ones being worse off. Many residents were forced to live upstairs, and one resident had to fit a platform in the kitchen so that food could be prepared without having to stand in the icy cold water. Another resident, who said she was better off than many as she only had 8 to 10 in of water in the house, was able to light a fire and sit by it with her relatives over Christmas, their feet on a raised plank to keep them out of the

The Wilton Address presented to King Edward VII on his visit to the town, 27 June 1908

The 1910 floods

water. Conditions were also made even more unpleasant because both front and back doors had to be left open day and night. They had been banked up with boards and turves in an effort to try to keep the water out.

The flooding virtually cut the town in two between the east and the west ends, and staging had to be erected over pathways to allow pedestrians to get from one side to the other. The town council helped by hiring a wagonette, which they put into service to convey people through the floodwater free of charge. The flooding lasted just over four days, subsiding almost as quickly as it had arrived, but the unfortunate householders spent many more weeks mopping up and trying to dry out their homes. There was more serious flooding in the town in 1915. This time the North Street area was most affected, and here again the depth of water was able to support a boat in places.

The Medical Officer of Health for Wilton estimated in a report of 1911 that the population of the town and urban district had increased by the midsummer of the previous year to 2,371 by natural increment, and that by his estimate, the census due to be taken later in this year would show that this was in excess of the actual number. In 1901 the census figure had shown that the population was 2,203, and since then there had been 168 more births than deaths registered. It was also reported that the number of inhabited houses was 551, with the average number of inmates being 4.3 persons. When the census returns were announced it was revealed that the

The December 1910 General Election coincided with the floods in Wilton

Pupils of an infants class at the National School, West Street, *c.* 1912

population had decreased by 79 since 1901, and that it now stood at 2,124. According to the report there had been an outbreak of scarlatina, with 50 cases reported. This had spread due to the fact that early cases had only been mild, and children had still attended school when symptoms were not so noticeable. As a result, many of the later cases had been very severe. To curtail the disease, the town's nurse was employed to see that isolation and disinfection was properly carried out, and this had the desired effect of limiting the outbreak.

With the increase in traffic, roads through the town were causing problems. Pedestrians complained that cars travelling through the town centre were covering them in dust. Other outlying areas had already asphalted their roads and, according to the mayor, Wilton was way behind in this matter. He saw no reason why Wilton should not experiment in asphalting roads, especially as the gas works had an abundant supply of tar, the use of which would cut costs considerably.

Attempts were also made to limit the speed of cars through the town to 10 miles per hour, as excessive speeds were causing a nuisance and damage, as well as causing concern to the public. There had apparently been cases reported of cars speeding down Shaftesbury Road at 40 miles per hour, 'a positive danger to children'.

May 1912 saw the opening of the recreation ground, developed on what had been a piece of waste ground known as the Hop Gardens, owned by the Wilton Estate and at the entrance to the town from Salisbury. The estate had leased the land to the council, who decided that it should be developed as a playground for children as well as an area of peace and quiet for those who wished to either walk or sit by the river. The area was developed as a memorial to King Edward VII and was paid for by public subscription, although the scheme was not too popular with a number of people in the town. In the early days the money was slow coming in, so much so that the committee which had been formed to oversee the project got into debt. A new committee was formed, and with the help of the council the project came to fruition despite the apathy and resentment of many Wiltonians who were still against the idea. The ground had been laid out by men from Lord Pembroke's estate along with council workmen, all of whom worked under the direction of the Head Gardener of Wilton House, Mr T. Challis. At the opening ceremony Lord Pembroke paid tribute to all those who had been connected with the scheme, and he afterwards performed a second ceremony which had been combined with the opening, when he presented a certificate and medal, plus a watch and a cup, to James Henry Sanger. A Wilton resident, Mr Sanger had received this honour in recognition of his brave attempt to try to save the life of his friend, who had fallen over the low

The recreation ground before the bowling green was laid down

parapet of a bridge into a swollen river at midnight the previous December. Although unsuccessful in his gallant attempt, Mr Sanger received his award thanks to suggestions made in the local press.

August 1914 saw the outbreak of the First World War, and a large number of troops encamped in the surrounding area. There was a small military camp situated at the bottom of the Fair Field near to the crossroads in the Avenue, and local troops used Grovely Woods for training exercises. As a result of the military camps in the area, train operations at the LSWR station became extra busy, especially with the handling of goods traffic. To accommodate this increase, two extra sidings were added to the Fair Field.

It was as a result of these heavy shunting operations that a rather spectacular accident occurred at the station on the morning of Saturday 7 August 1915, between an Exeter-bound express train and three goods trucks, which had inadvertently been left on the main line in its path. As the express train rounded the curve, the driver saw the trucks on the line in front of him, but because of his speed he was unable to stop in time. He crashed into the trucks which were loaded with barrels of tar, and the force of the impact sent trucks and barrels hurtling into the air, landing on the platform. The barrels spilt their contents over platform, tracks and engine. Luckily the train was slowing down and was not even derailed. It eventually came to a stop at the far end of the platform.

Market Cross and the original market place

There were fortunately no deaths or serious injuries, and only three people needed medical treatment. The local doctor was summoned to the scene, but the injured had only sustained cuts of a minor nature, one soldier having cut his head as he jumped from the train when it was moving. He had been looking out of the window, observing what was about to happen.

There was a friendly invasion of Australian troops in the area as the war progressed. Many were stationed at Hurdcot Camp in the Wylye valley, often visiting the town when off duty and making friends with the residents. A Miss Uphill from West Street befriended many of them, and she even opened a special room in South Street where all soldiers could go for relaxation. This became known as 'Miss Uphill's Dugout', and it was situated in the building which now houses the library. She even wrote a long letter, published in the *Brisbane Daily Mail*, in which she spoke lovingly of the Australian soldiers. She mentioned how much they enjoyed the beauty of the surrounding countryside, made a fuss of the children and were courteous to women, and remembered in particular that they never scrambled into cars before the ladies were seated.

News of the ending of the war was greeted in the town with great relief. The bells of the parish church rang out, townspeople decorated their houses

Miss Uphill's soldiers 'rest room', known locally as the 'dugout' during the First World War

with flags and bunting, and flocked to the market place, where the mayor announced that an armistice had been signed and hostilities had ceased. The mayor paid tribute to the Army, Navy and women workers, as well as to all the others who had played a part in attaining this happy result. In the evening a short thanksgiving service was held in the parish church, and a much larger service was held the following Sunday.

Wilton started to get back to normal and made efforts to pick up the pieces of its peacetime pursuits. There was a regular train service to Salisbury, but buses now offered a similar service and were very well patronized, despite the rather bumpy ride as a result of their solid tyres. In 1920 Wiltshire and Dorset Motor Services started operating between Wilton and Salisbury via Harnham Bridge, using open-topped double deckers. The service from Wilton ran from Market Square, and in 1921 Wiltshire and Dorset Motor Services bought out a rival company called Salisbury and District Motor Services. In 1922 another rival company, the Victory Motor Services, started to operate, but only existed until 1933 when it was taken over by Wiltshire and Dorset Motor Services. In February 1921 the town council decided that all motor buses running between Salisbury and Wilton using the stand in the market place should be charged an annual rental of £2 per bus, and that the present agreement between the council and Wiltshire and Dorset Motor Services should be terminated.

A Wilts and Dorset bus in the market place waiting to return to Salisbury, late 1930s

In May 1924 the enhancement of the market place was completed when the memorial to Sidney, 14th Earl of Pembroke, was unveiled by Lord Radnor at a ceremony attended by the mayor and corporation, who had been recommended to attend by a special committee. This was due to the fact that the memorial was to be handed over to the corporation in perpetuity.

The enhancement scheme in the town centre had been drafted prior to the First World War, as the area had become run down. During the war, however, the buildings were commandeered by the military. The rents obtained provided appreciable additional funds for the memorial, which already had funds donated by relatives and friends of the late earl and residents of the town. The earl had been a former mayor of the borough, as well as a one-time MP for Wilton.

Between 1918 and 1920 buildings including the wool loft, which stood on the corner of North Street and Silver Street, were demolished and the site cleared to extend the market place. At the same time this brought about the demise of Brede Street. Plans were made to place the memorial in the centre of this new area.

Unveiling the Pembroke Memorial in the market place, May 1924

The market place, showing a Wilts & Dorset bus waiting to return to Salisbury, late 1920s

South Street, showing the old loft at the end of the street on the right. The building was demolished after the First World War to make way for the new market place

The Wilton gas works had been in some financial trouble around this time, but by early 1925 it was starting to make a profit, brought about by having its affairs put on a proper business footing. The mayor reported at a council meeting that the coal being used could now be paid for immediately, and made them eligible for a discount on purchase. A reserve fund had been set up for larger pipework to be installed in Shaftesbury Road, to supply gas to new houses that were being built there. Now that profits were being achieved, customers benefited from reductions in price.

A housing committee report in 1927 revealed that tenders for the Fair Field site reserved for houses had been £100 less than the government valuer had recommended for private housing. It was suggested that the council should build council-houses on the site, charging a reasonable rent. This type of housing was urgently needed and it was felt that with average wages of between 30s. and 35s. a week many people could not afford to pay high rents. With average rents in the region of 8s. a week, it was considered that this was about the maximum people could afford. There were already 28 council-houses in use in Fairview Road and a further 36 in Wishford Road. Later in the 1930s the council increased its housing stock with 30 new houses in the Hollows, and a further 8 in Victoria Road.

Arthur Street, a tenant farmer at Ditchampton Farm, achieved fame as an author when his first book, *Farmers Glory*, was published in 1932. The original manuscript was written in pencil in some old grocery books. However, Arthur's writing career had started earlier, when he had written an angry article on farming which was published in the *Daily Mail*. Amazed at the amount of payment he received for its publication, he got the bug for writing, and regular columns by him began appearing in the *Salisbury Times* and *Farmers Weekly*. It was during this period that he was encouraged by Edith Olivier to write *Farmers Glory*, and despite the effort of having to write after a heavy day's work on the farm, it proved to be well worth his while. It was an instant success on publication, and became a best-seller. Encouraged by this success, he went on to write many more books with farming themes, and also became a household name in broadcasting. He is best remembered as a regular member of the panel on *Any Questions*, his Wiltshire accent and wit becoming a feature of the programme.

In 1951 he relinquished the tenancy of Ditchampton Farm, on which he had been born in 1892. He took up the tenancy of Mill Farm, which lies on the opposite side of the Wylye valley, and which, like the farm at Ditchampton, was owned by the Wilton Estate.

The lawns at Wilton House were the setting for a large pageant and seventeenth-century fair for two days in June 1933, celebrating the tercentenary of George Herbert, Rector of Bemerton. The pageant, which consisted of four separate episodes containing several scenes in each, took about three hours to perform, with intervals between each episode. The seventeenth-century fair was set up in the area between the main gate and the house, and a great deal of trouble was taken by the organizers to reproduce items as near as possible to the period. Some of these items included authentic recipes of cordials and essences, sweets, cakes and children's toys. Children's games – shuttlecock, titter totter and a jingling match – were played, and other attractions were the tobacco man, an ale booth, stocks, and boys playing marbles.

A major event in the town in 1935 was the celebration of the Silver Jubilee of King George V. The residents celebrated in their customary fashion, but this time there was also a carnival procession and a confetti battle. Also in 1935 was the opening of the new Wilton Senior Mixed School in the Hollows.

The school was provided by the Church of England authorities at a cost of £9,000, and when it was opened it accommodated 177 boys and girls from Wilton and 8 from surrounding parishes. There were 5 forms, and an allowance was made for each class to have 40 pupils. The aim of the school's curriculum was to embrace subjects which were beyond the scope of the

Some of the entrants for the carnival procession held to celebrate the Silver Jubilee of George V in 1935

normal elementary school. Children who lived outside the parish in South Newton, Wishford and Netherhampton had to cycle to school each day on machines provided by the educational authorities, and for the children from Burcombe, Barford St Martin, Compton Chamberlayne, Dinton and Teffont, a special bus service was provided. Pupils also received a third of a pint of milk a day at a cost of ½d. and hot lunches, consisting of two courses, costing 3d. a day. The school in West Street reverted to catering for juniors and infants, and the only other school in the town was a private one in North Street. Both the Wilton Park School and the Free School were no longer in existence, having closed in 1920 and 1923 respectively.

History was made at the council meeting in November 1938, when Miss Edith Olivier was elected to office as Wilton's first lady mayor. She was the daughter of Canon Dacres Olivier, a former rector of the town for many years. Edith Olivier was a popular choice as she was loved by everyone in

Wilton area Church of England Senior Mixed School, opened September 1935

the town, and she loved them and spent hours of her busy life helping all those who were less fortunate than herself. She was also an authoress, having written many books which contained her observations of life and personalities in Wilton during her younger years. In her acceptance speech she spoke of the new housing scheme that was being proposed, saying that it would not only provide comfortable houses for the inhabitants, but would not in any way diminish the beauty of the surroundings. For the monthly meetings of the council she announced that she would wear her mayoral gown, as she felt this would add to her presence, both physically and morally, but she added that she did not expect the councillors to wear their gowns.

Her caring nature was shown on the last day of the year when she revived the custom of distributing bread from the doorway of the old church in the market place. In letters sent to the recipients of this old charitable function, she reminded them of how this gift had been started about a hundred years previously by people who had cared about those less fortunate than themselves. They had made the request that bread should be given on New Year's Day at the church. In her letter, she said that she wanted to act in memory of these people. Miss Olivier concluded by saying that it was apt that she should be reviving the custom as Wilton's first lady mayor, as the word 'lady' is derived from an ancient word meaning 'loaf giver'.

St Mary's viewed from Kingsbury Square

As the year came to a close, the threat of war was in the air and already preparations were being made in case the threat became a reality. Wiltonians waiting to greet the New Year were wondering how war, if it came, would affect their lives, and what sacrifices they might have to make.

CHAPTER FIVE

1939–45

Because of the threat of war, Wilton council in 1939 was fully engaged in drawing up plans that would be put into operation in the event of hostilities. Of major local interest among these plans was one for adapting the Talbot & Wyvern Hall for use as an ARP first-aid post.

This plan, however, was causing some confusion, due to the fact that it could not be fully established who was to be responsible for the adaptation of the hall. The town clerk had written a letter asking for a straight 'yes' or 'no' as to whether Wilton or the county was responsible, but the reply he received was, in his opinion, rather ambiguous. Many of the councillors who read it thought it indicated that the county was responsible, and suggested that they went ahead with the plans on those lines, at the same time informing the county ARP committee of their decision.

In a letter to the townspeople, the mayor said that she had been deputed to assist the government in the preparation and completion of a scheme for the evacuation of civilian populations from danger zones in times of war, and she appealed for assistance to carry out this duty. The council engaged volunteer workers to make house-to-house calls, in order to obtain a detailed estimate of the number of persons that could be accommodated in the borough in an emergency. A pamphlet was distributed at the same time explaining the scheme, in which it said that the council knew that the people of Wilton would play their part, as in the past, in helping their country, should the need arise. At the same time the mayor made arrangements with the rector for a bell to be rung at the church every day at midday to remind people from all religious denominations to pray for peace.

Already the town had been successful in obtaining fifteen volunteers as air-raid wardens, but there was an urgent need to double this number. The ARP scheme had been discussed in great detail by the council and had been passed to the county council for approval, but there were delays in getting the scheme together. Because of this, Wilton was the last authority in the county to send off its proposals.

Despite the anxiety of the possibility of war, life in the town continued as normally as possible. One of the main concerns was still traffic problems,

Kingsbury Square, showing the Talbot & Wyvern Hall in the background to the left, early 1900s

especially at the bottleneck of Silver Street and West Street. Plans had been made to ease this situation, and three possible schemes had been suggested. One was to remove the town hall, thereby widening the bottleneck, or to go a little further and take off a corner of Kingsbury Square, widening the road between the bank and Harwood's shop on the other side of the market place. A committee report said that the scheme for the Fugglestone housing site had been approved by the Ministry of Health. The number of houses allocated for rehousing and slum clearance would be 38, for rehousing through overcrowding 6, and for general requirements 8, making a total of 52 new houses in all for the town.

The rehallowing of the chancel of the old church of St Mary's in the market place, plus the dedication of the churchyard, which was to be an open space of quietness, took place on 6 May. The ceremony was performed by the bishop of the diocese. A memorial tablet was dedicated to Robert Bingham, Bishop of Salisbury, who was consecrated here in 1229, and to Robert Bingham, the US ambassador. It was unveiled by the Rt Hon. George Charles Bingham. The event was the result of a visit made to Wilton by the late Robert Bingham when he was US ambassador. He discovered that an ancestor had been consecrated here, and offered to restore the building as a memorial to him. Unfortunately he died before the work could be put in hand, but other members of his family agreed to have the work done as this had been his wish.

The threat of war was never far away, and preparation exercises continued in the town and surrounding area. One involved a blackout being imposed on

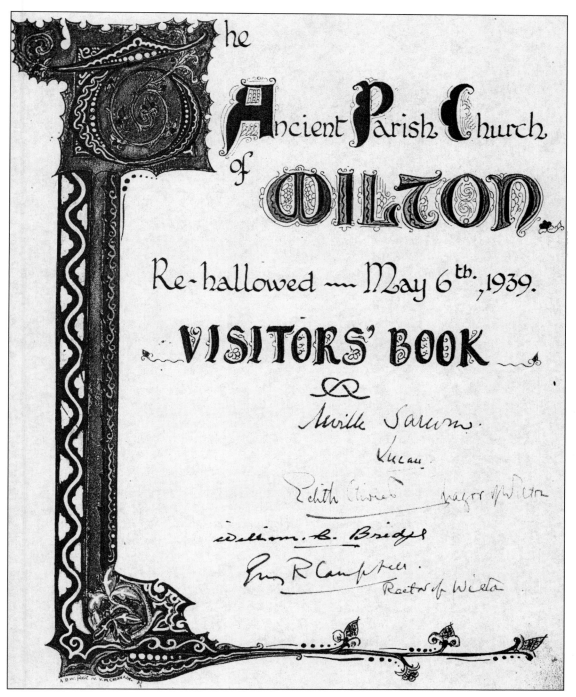

Signatures of the dignitaries attending the re-hallowing of the ancient parish church of St Mary's

the town from 10 p.m. to midnight, in order to simulate an air attack in which heavy losses were inflicted on the area, the imaginary targets being airfields and two aerodrome factories (one of the latter being represented by Wilton House). The exercise was run along lines that would prevail in a wartime situation, and was as realistic as possible. Everything seemed to go according to plan, and a Home Office representative was more than satisfied with the parts played by Wilton people.

Once war had been declared the town soon received its first group of evacuees, some of whom came from Court Lane School in Cosham, near Portsmouth. The children were in good spirits and scrambled off the coach clutching emergency rations and gas masks, the latter being somewhat of a novelty to the reception committee, as they had not yet been issued in Wilton. The children were aged between five and eleven years, and after being formally received by the mayor and mayoress, the Countess of Pembroke, the rector and his wife, plus a number of Wilton people, they were quickly taken to their billets by car. The next day another group was received, and soon settled down in their new surroundings.

Many newspapers carried complaints on the subject of evacuated children, but it appears that there were no such grumbles concerning Wilton, at least from the school in Cosham. Soon after the arrival of the children the mayor received a letter from all those concerned at the school, thanking her for the warm reception they had received, and for the admirable way in which householders had accommodated them.

Wilton became a main assembly point for troops, and the town was soon overwhelmed by them. At night they were forced to sleep in the felt mills, wool stores and anywhere else that could be provided at short notice. The Sheep Fair Field became one huge car-park for the storage of military vehicles, and the streets echoed to the sound of marching feet as soldiers passed through for guard duties. One of the most popular venues for those off duty was the Greydawn Café near the market place, where the proprietors were kept busy supplying sustenance to ever-hungry men.

Although things had not been going too well generally during this early period known as the 'phoney war', many people still remained preoccupied with their own affairs, not seeming to bother very much about the war. They changed their attitude in May 1940, when the Germans dropped parachutists into Belgium and rumours started to spread that some were even in this country, disguised as clergymen and nuns. It was now evident that the war was getting closer, so many residents started to get together, collecting hefty objects and even old guns which might come in useful in the event of an invasion. This led to the formation of the 'Local Defence Volunteers', later to become known as the Home Guard, who spent every minute they could afford training to defend the town. They received a number of invasion scares, which were fortunately false alarms. After one alarm which proved to be false, a local man was heard to remark, with typical Wiltshire wit, 'They Germans, they're not dependable – you can't rely on them for anything'.

An invasion committee had been formed and issued various directives to residents on what to do in the event of emergency. Water supplies were a priority, and in order for a sufficient supply to be conserved in the reservoir, water through the mains would only be supplied between the hours of 7 a.m. and 8 a.m. and from 5 p.m. to 6 p.m., during which time householders were instructed to fill jugs, kettles, basins, baths etc. When mains water was available its use was strictly limited to drinking, cooking and the preparation of food. Baths were to be curtailed, and for washing and flushing WCs, only the use of either rainwater or river water was permitted. Should the main supply be exhausted, it was thought to be safe to use river water, providing that it was boiled for three minutes. Similar instructions applied if the supply was cut as a result of enemy action, but for houses that were furthest from the rivers a limited supply would be brought in water carts. Residents living near rivers would have to obtain all their supplies from this source.

The Municipal Offices were moved from the town hall to Fugglestone House, situated in secluded grounds on the Wilton Road near the crossroads at the foot of the army camp. The camp was now the headquarters of Southern Command, but because of the importance that it was playing in wartime operations, it was decided by the military to move the main operational centre to Wilton House for greater security. The Earl and Countess of Pembroke continued to stay there, but in limited accommodation of just two or three rooms.

Edith Olivier remained mayoress until 1941, after which Sam Shergold took up office for the next twelve months. He was employed as an engine driver on the railway, so in order for him to perform his mayoral duties the railway allowed him to work a special night shift from midnight until 8 o'clock the next morning. At the end of his term of office, many councillors were engaged in full-time jobs and other important voluntary work, and it was impossible for them to take on the office of mayor. This duty fell to the Countess of Pembroke, and she remained in office until after the war.

Many sacrifices had to be made for the war effort in order for factories to be supplied with raw materials to manufacture tanks, aircraft and weapons. Iron railings were removed from many properties, including those which surrounded St Mary's church in the market place. Besides material items, money was also required, and in conjunction with Salisbury and the surrounding district, Wilton joined in with a special War Weapons Week.

West Street, late 1930s. The rails in front of the house on the right were removed during the Second World War

On the first day, the mayors of Wilton and Salisbury broadcast to each other from their respective town halls, being relayed at the same time to a large crowd in the market place. Later there was a fly past of bomber aircraft over the town, and a special exhibition of ancient and modern war weapons was organized in the town hall. Many other events were held during the week, including a procession of mechanized military vehicles, plus soldiers from surrounding military camps, the Home Guard and civil defence workers. After the procession the vehicles were on display in the market place. A special drive for the selling of War Bonds and National Saving Certificates was also launched.

One of the main dangers in war is fire from enemy air attacks, and during an alert in 1940 some incendiary bonds were dropped just inside Wilton Park near Netherhampton. Fortunately there were no casualties and very little damage was reported. On another occasion a similar attack was made on a train passing over the bridge in Warminster Road. Fortunately the train was not hit, the bombs falling on the embankment and making a few small holes and scorch marks in the grass. As a result, two hundred volunteers of both sexes were organized into fire-watching parties, enabling any fires which did

Fugglestone House, used by the town council as offices during the Second World War and for the wartime broadcast in February 1943

break out to be quickly dealt with by the fire brigade. This matter was considered to be of exceptional importance, and everyone was asked to share in this work.

With invasion still being a possibility, Wilton residents were given an opportunity to find out for themselves just what would be required of them if such an invasion took place. This experience took the form of a special exercise one weekend in September 1942, which also involved Salisbury, Downton, Netherhampton and Quidhampton. The exercise was very realistic and the civilian population was asked to cooperate fully with the tasks that would be asked of them by the military, police, civil defence and other organizations. Places of entertainment, licensed premises and shops were all closed at 4 p.m. on the Saturday, and all transport facilities ceased. Various problematic situations were created in nearly every street. These had to be dealt with solely by the inhabitants, and on that Saturday night very few residents had any sleep. Thankfully, none of these plans was ever needed.

An interesting observation was made by an American broadcaster visiting Wilton in February 1943. He was taking part in a broadcast by the BBC in conjunction with the Columbia Broadcasting System of America, which was to be transmitted live from Fugglestone House. After his arrival at the southern station, which had all signs removed as a security precaution, he heard the sound of children singing as he turned into North Street. It came from a small private school which had a thatched roof and white walls. The peace was suddenly shattered when some British tanks on manoeuvres roared round the corner and drowned out the singing. At the same time, two planes flew low over the centre of the town and the surrounding hills started to boom with the sound of gunfire. The American later summed up the situation perfectly in his broadcast, when he described the scene as 'The noise of war – breaking up the song of peace'.

During his short visit he found the residents friendly, and he met many of them in the shops. There was one shop in particular which fascinated him, Partridges the newsagents. He described it as being small and rather dark, with a few newspapers and magazines on a shelf and a small glass counter, on which were displayed bottles of ink, pens and pencils. At the rear of the counter there were tobaccos and cigarettes, while another area of the shop was taken up with packets of notepaper and envelopes, all mixed with combs and hair slides, plus a jar of sweets. He was most surprised to learn that although he was in a newsagents, it was impossible for him to buy a newspaper. He was politely informed that the reason was due to a wartime regulation to save paper, resulting in newspapers being rationed to regular customers only.

By now people had adapted their lives to wartime conditions, as well as to shortages, rationing and many other restrictions that were prevailing. Despite these changes everyone tried to carry on with life as normally as possible. Production of carpets had ceased at the carpet factory, owing to the shortage of wool, but the factory was saved from bankruptcy by taking on work for the military, washing blankets. Starting off with only a small number, the factory eventually dealt with ten thousand a week. Extra revenue was earned by garnishing camouflage and making kitbags and tarpaulins.

Bishopstone Hill became a useful area for storing and maintaining army vehicles, its avenue of trees hiding them from aerial attack. For maintenance purposes inspection pits were provided. One of these still remains to this day. Grovely Woods was out of bounds to the general public, as they were used for the storing of ammunition and bombs, once again trees offering an effective camouflage from the air. New roads were built to accommodate the hundreds of lorries transporting these items and many new paths were made, which today benefit visitors to the woods. However, since the war many have become covered in earth and leaves, making them difficult to find.

Although the people had been well prepared for the invasion that had looked likely to come from Germany, they were not really prepared for the invasion of American troops which Wilton experienced not long after the USA entered the war. The US troops were based at Southern Command and they certainly livened up the town. Their jeeps, in particular, seemed to be everywhere, darting about all over the place. It seemed that nearly every American soldier had one of his own. At least this invasion was friendly, and on the whole the town's residents welcomed the Americans. There were some, however, who were not so keen on their presence, objecting to what they termed 'their brash, gum-chewing manner'. They had not, of course, experienced the shortages that the British had, and to children they were particularly kind, often giving them packets of American chewing-gum. These were eagerly received, as sweets were in short supply and on ration.

In the spring of 1942 there were two air-raid alerts in Wilton in one night. Waves of bombers flew near to the town, and some bombs dropped not far away. It seems the main attack was on Bath, and so serious that the Wilton fire engine was called to assist with fire-fighting and other operations, along with others from the area.

Wilton was surviving the war, but everyone in the town knew that it was never far away. Southampton was a regular target of German bombers. It might have been only twenty-two miles away, but at night-time, when the raids were taking place, it seemed much nearer. From many bedroom windows in Wilton a huge orange glow could be seen over Southampton in the dark sky. Perhaps being under the umbrella of Southern Command, and the sight of soldiers in the streets made Wiltonians feel safer, even though the enemy could have caused untold damage if they had decided to bomb Wilton House.

It was fortunate that such an incident never took place. If it had the D-Day landings would have been badly affected, and might not have taken place when they did. The reason was that for many months prior to the landings, much planning had taken place in the Double Cube Room of Wilton House. The paintings, carefully protected, were covered with maps of the beaches of France, and behind the walls of the grounds many secret exercises took place. Thankfully, when the landings took place on 6 June 1944, they did help to bring the war in Europe to an end. On the night prior to the landings there was an almost constant drone of aircraft flying overhead, lasting about seven hours and keeping many people in Wilton awake. They were able to witness this great Armada of the sky, lit by red and blue lights.

Entertainment for troops in Wilton was very limited. Salisbury was the main venue, catering for servicemen's needs in their off-duty hours, but Wilton did occasionally put on concerts and dances. Realizing there was a great need for better entertainment facilities in the town, the Wilton Allied Forces Centre was opened in June 1944. It was built on a site provided by the British Army. The two buildings covered 3,000 sq ft of floor space. They included a hall which could seat two hundred people, in addition to a library

The market place in the late 1940s, showing the Pembroke Memorial

and discussion and reading rooms. The entertainments available were to include films, drama, concerts and other activities, including photography, music, lectures and art, all supported by the Council for Encouragement of Music and the Arts.

Early in May 1945 the war with Germany ended, and the people in Wilton, like those in every other town, city and village, celebrated the end of hostilities with thankful hearts and great relief. In the town all the flags that residents could muster were hung from windows, pennants of red, white and blue fluttered in the streets, and a huge Union Jack was hung from the parish church.

Despite pouring rain, large crowds gathered in the market place to hear the prime minister's speech relayed by loudspeaker. Afterwards the crowd, made up of servicemen and women, American soldiers and civilians (many of whom were young children), witnessed the sounding of the ceasefire by the buglers of the Scots Guards. Simultaneously the rain clouds broke, bathing the market place in brilliant sunshine, an impressive sight to herald a new era of peace.

In the evening large crowds gathered once again in the market place to hear the king's speech, after which Wiltonians indulged in their love of torchlight processions. Two thousand of them, along with fifty torch-bearers, made their way to Grovely Down. Here there was a huge bonfire, erected by German prisoners-of-war who had been held in a small camp at the top of the Shaftesbury Road, opposite the cemetery. It is said that they were not happy to erect this bonfire in celebration of the defeat of their country. The

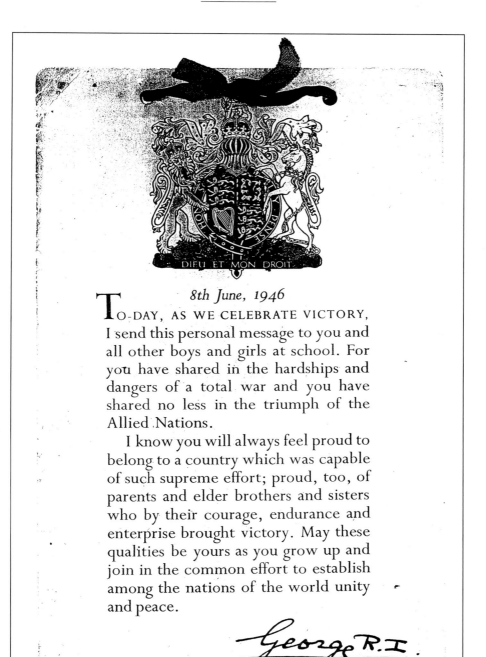

8th June, 1946

To-day, as we celebrate victory, I send this personal message to you and all other boys and girls at school. For you have shared in the hardships and dangers of a total war and you have shared no less in the triumph of the Allied Nations.

I know you will always feel proud to belong to a country which was capable of such supreme effort; proud, too, of parents and elder brothers and sisters who by their courage, endurance and enterprise brought victory. May these qualities be yours as you grow up and join in the common effort to establish among the nations of the world unity and peace.

George R.I

Victory message sent to local schoolchildren from King George VI

War memorial in the churchyard of the parish church, on which are inscribed the names of Wilton men who lost their lives in both world wars

lighting ceremony was performed by the Countess of Pembroke and an American officer. The blaze eventually became so great that it could be seen easily at Harnham. A radio van was also at the scene, relaying music to which people danced and rejoiced until well past midnight.

Wilton had come safely through the war, despite anxious times in the early days. But in those times Arthur Street did have faith that Wilton would survive, and during the broadcast from Fugglestone House in 1943, he delivered a message in an almost Churchillian manner, informing the country and America that Wilton would survive. He said we put our faith in the future in our children, hoping that they would once again see sheep fairs and pleasure fairs, knowing that there were no guns in the hills and no tanks that might come round the corner. He also wanted them to enjoy the pleasures of the country and in conclusion, said that although the war had come to Wilton, making its mark on everyone, we would survive and Wilton would survive. Wilton has lived between its chalky streams longer than the Kingdom of England itself.

Now Wilton was able to apply its energies to more peaceful pursuits. The long weary years of war could not be wiped away overnight, however, and the community spirit that had prevailed in wartime would still be needed in the times ahead.

CHAPTER SIX

1946–50

Wilton was starting to recover from the war, but it was a slow recovery. There were still shortages of many everyday items, and rationing was still in force. Most men who had served in the war had returned, but sadly there were others who had not. They were not to be forgotten, and arrangements were soon made to have their names carved on the war memorial in the churchyard, along with those of men who had lost their lives in the First World War.

German prisoners-of-war had been repatriated, and the buildings in which they had been held were converted to house displaced persons from Europe – from Poland, Hungary, Yugoslavia and the Ukraine. Many of these unfortunate people were employed locally on a voluntary basis, in return for being looked after.

Clubs and societies started to flourish once again, and the Wilton Musical and Dramatic Society boasted ninety members. They could not wait to get started, and at their Annual General Meeting in March 1946, under the chairmanship of the rector, they made ambitious plans to mount at least two productions a year. In the summer they decided that one would take place outdoors and most likely be a play by Shakespeare, while later in the year, just before Christmas, there would be something suitable for the festive season.

Although there were spontaneous celebrations immediately after the war ended, official celebrations did not take place until June 1946. One of the main reasons for this delay was that prior to the end of the war, the council had decided that official celebrations should not take place until the war with Japan had ceased. The original celebrations had been only for the victory in Europe.

On the day of the celebrations heavy rain persisted throughout the morning and afternoon, causing a few anxious moments for the organizers and eventually leading to the postponement of the sports. Fortunately, by the evening the rain had cleared sufficiently to allow a carnival procession to parade through the town, which proved to be a huge success. As darkness fell another procession formed, leaving just after 10 o'clock to march through the streets before arriving at its destination at the top of the Avenue. Here there was a huge bonfire and firework display. The crowd was witnessing the first public display of fireworks made by WAE Co. (now Paynes Wessex) at their Woodford factory. This company had not long been released from its wartime work of 'smoke' manufacturing.

The mayor was up in arms later in the year over some remarks that had been made by a local farmer to the National Farmers' Union. He had suggested that the Britford Sheep Fair should be held in Salisbury, as in his opinion facilities at Wilton were not very good. The mayor took great exception to these remarks and replied by saying that although Britford Fair was shortly to be dissolved, it was most unfortunate that such remarks should be made about Wilton. In the mayor's opinion, backed by the council, it was stressed that Wilton Fair had never been inferior and compared with Salisbury the town had better road and rail links. It was also pointed out that when the fair at Salisbury was closed for a period, Wilton had offered its facilities which had been gratefully accepted.

The start of 1947 brought a spell of very severe weather, consisting of heavy falls of snow and arctic conditions. Added to all this misery were power cuts and drastic shortages of all kinds of fuel, but the resolve of Wilton's residents was not broken. As in the war, they made the best of their situation, helping each other with that important ingredient, community spirit.

An announcement was made by Southern Command that it would not be too long before it would completely vacate Wilton House, returning it fully to the Earl of Pembroke. It was hoped that this would happen by the end of the year, or early in the following year at the latest. At that time only the ground floor was occupied, mainly by the GOC-in-Chief, the Chief of Staff and some other officers.

In August the town council took its first tentative steps to provide playing fields in the town, the site of Castle Meadows in North Street having already been chosen. While the council was prepared to purchase the meadows, it decided that any equipment required would have to be paid for by public subscription, as even after the purchase price had been paid it would be involved in further expenditure raising the ground. The need to raise the ground level was important because the area was meadowland, prone to flooding during winter months.

The carpet factory was now back in full production, orders were coming in and the weavers were once again busy operating the looms and producing high quality handmade carpets, just as they had done prior to the war. In 1948 they completed an order for the Empire Theatre in London's Leicester Square, with a carpet made in one piece measuring 23 ft 4 in by 39 ft 6 in for use in the lower foyer. The felt mills were also in full production, their hooter becoming quite a familiar sound in the town. Because it only operated at certain times of the day, it unofficially became Wilton's second clock.

North Street from the market place with St Mary's church on the right, early 1900s. The first building on the left with the sunblinds was the former Greydawn Café, now Barclays Bank

One very popular annual event was the Whit Monday Fête, organized by the parish church and held in the rectory garden. This was a perfect setting with its long lawn lined with tall hedges and trees, stretching down to the river. Lines of trestle tables were covered with a large selection of items for sale, ranging from bath salts and mouth-watering home-made cakes, to toys, tinned foods, and old magazines and comics. The latter were usually neatly rolled and tied with string at 2d. a bundle. Always included in the sideshows was bowling for a pig, and other attractions included donkey rides, a fortune teller, gymnastic displays and country dancing. One year these attractions included a boxing display given by the boys from the Bishop Wordsworth School in Salisbury. Baby shows were also popular, the contestants dressed up in their finery, and being carefully weighed by the town's nurse. Ascents of the church tower were well patronized, and after the long climb to the top, the curious were rewarded with magnificent views across the town, nestled comfortably in tree-lined rolling downland. One feature which completed these occasions was amplified music of popular tunes of the day, played on rather scratchy 78 r.p.m. records, occasionally interrupted by announcements of events and features.

View of West Street after the Second World War

Although Wilton is only a small market town, there was an abundance of shops catering for practically every need at this time, among them seven grocers (including a Co-operative Stores in the market place and an International Stores in North Street). Further down that street was a drapers selling all kinds of items, from haberdashery to ladies' attire, with the men's department in another shop further down on the opposite side of the street. Other shops included three butchers, two newsagents, bakers, sweet shops, a fishmongers and many more, too numerous to mention. The shops were well patronized by Wilton residents, but many people came in from villages in the Wylye and Nadder valleys, finding it more convenient to shop here than in Salisbury.

Council housing became a prime concern, and plans to build new homes were put in hand. Preliminary discussions had already taken place in November 1944, when the town council had made tentative plans to purchase 10 acres of land from the Wilton Estate in the Wishford Road. The plan was to build twenty-five houses in the first year after the war, and a further twenty-five the following year.

After discussions with Wilton Estate, agreement was reached and land purchased in the middle of Ditchampton Farm, much to the annoyance of the tenant farmer, Arthur Street. He made protests that building houses on that site would render the farm an unworkable holding, causing maximum

An aerial view of the town, taken between the wars, looking towards the market place

harm to farming and the minimum of benefit to the town. His protest turned out to be in vain, despite efforts made on his behalf by the Ministry of Agriculture, who were forced to give way. The council had tried to find two alternative sites, but although they were ideal in that they were situated nearer to the town, with all main services laid on, the sites were turned down by government departments. This left the council no alternative but to commence building on the site at Ditchampton Farm. Included in the development were a number of Reema-type houses, built in sections which locked together. Not only were they quicker to build, they were also thought to be much easier to maintain, and hopefully would cut the costs of future repairs. The council also provided some emergency accommodation at Fugglestone with the erection of some prefabricated buildings, all of which remained occupied for many years longer than planned.

There was a frequent bus service to Salisbury, as well as to many of the outlying villages, and both stations provided regular train services. Most of the town's traders received their goods by rail and coal traffic was particularly heavy, with truckloads coming in every week. Travellers could buy tickets from here to any destination in the country and good use was made of all the local stopping services. During summer months at the Southern station there was heavy traffic in lettuces, all of which would be hastily despatched to the shops so that they could be sold in farm-fresh condition.

In the summer of 1947 the Southern station made railway history when it was used for changing the engines on the *Devon Belle*. This was an all-Pullman service running between Waterloo and Exeter, in theory non stop. As there were no water troughs provided on the route a change of engine was required, a practice normally carried out at Salisbury. As this was not an official stop it was decided that Wilton would be ideal. Another factor in this move was that it would avoid confusion with passengers at Salisbury. On the first Saturday of the *Devon Belle*'s run, many people flocked to the station to see the train, and many more were in Wishford Road to watch it pass over the bridge. The practice of changing engines at Wilton remained until the demise of the train in the summer of 1954.

With the nationalization of the railways in 1949, both stations at Wilton received a change of name. British Railways decided that to have two stations on different routes with the same name would be confusing. It was decided that the former GWR station would be named Wilton North, and Wilton South would be the name given to the other. Apart from these new official names, both stations retained the identity of their previous owners. At Wilton North early in the following year a rail crash was averted due to the quick thinking of the station master. He saw an army lorry strike one of the pillars on the Kingsway Bridge, and debris from the demolished pillar fell onto the

The *Devon Belle* arriving at Wilton. A replacement engine waits in the siding

line. A Brighton to Cardiff express train was shortly to depart from Salisbury and pass through the station, so he quickly telephoned Salisbury and explained the situation. Fortunately his action was just in time to prevent the express leaving Salisbury, and a disaster was averted.

By August 1949 the Senior School in Wilton had received a change of name, becoming the Wilton Area Secondary Modern School. With the change of name there was also a change of headmaster, brought about by the retirement of the former one due to ill-health. In this month a special meeting was chaired by Lord Pembroke at which the managers of the secondary school were present, together with their counterparts from all the junior schools in parishes who were sending, or likely to send, children to the Wilton school.

The meeting was held to discuss the enlargement of, and improvements to, the secondary school, the cost of which was revealed by the County Director of Education to be in the region of £80,000. Half of this sum was to be provided by the Local Education Authority, but it was stressed that if the school was to retain its full status as a church-aided school, the remainder of the money would have to be raised by voluntary effort. A definite offer was received by the Director of Religious Education on behalf of the Diocese, who said it would contribute all but £12,000 of this latter sum, and that if each interested parish was prepared to contribute its proportionate share of the £12,000, Wilton's quota would be £3,000. However, the parishes thought that this amount was beyond their resources, although they did appreciate the Diocese's offer. The decision was made to explore alternative schemes before applying for what was known as controlled status.

In order to try to promote the town's trade and industry, Wilton Industrial Exhibition was held at the town hall for two days. All the town's firms that were engaged in local crafts and industry displayed their wares to the many hundreds of people who passed through the doors. During the exhibition period there were conducted tours round the carpet factory.

At the council offices (which were now housed in new premises, a former Masonic Hall in Kingsbury Square), there was an exhibition of the town archives, including some documents recently discovered when an old chest was opened. A tailor's dummy was put to good use displaying the uniform of the former Free School, and in the Mayor's Parlour one corner was devoted to some items of the late Edith Olivier, including a chair cover she had made, an antique needlework table and some of her books.

Edith Olivier had died in May the previous year, having suffered three strokes, and at her funeral in the parish church a large congregation, including the mayor and corporation, heard the rector pay glowing tributes to her life and work in the community. During her life she had made many friends who

Aerial view of the parish church showing the National School situated opposite in West Street

often stayed at her home, Daye House in Wilton Park. Among them were many well-known personalities of the day, including Cecil Beaton, Siegfried Sassoon, Lord David Cecil and the composer William Walton. Undoubtedly one of her best and closest friends was Rex Whistler, an artist who illustrated some of her books. When he was killed on active service during the war Edith was devastated.

In September 1949 the town council organized a carnival in order to raise money to help with the purchase of equipment for the playing fields in Castle Meadow. Some progress had been made towards the purchase of the land, but nothing had yet been finalized and it was still quite a way off.

The council received a huge response from residents for the week-long event. Houses, shops and streets were decorated, and everyone entered into the spirit. On the first Saturday a crowd of two thousand people flocked to a flag-bedecked market place to see the crowning of Phyllis Turner, Wilton's first Carnival Queen, who was accompanied by a page and four other attendants. The crown was an exact replica of those worn by Wessex kings. It was made by Mr Horace Uphill, a cabinet-maker and expert in antique furniture, whose business was in West Street. It only took him a week to make the crown, fashioning it out of aluminium and wood. It was trimmed with ermine and had a fringe studded with rock crystals, imitation pearls, emeralds and turquoise, lined with red velvet. The

A Wilton carnival. Men from Naish's felt mills with their firm's old fire pump about to take part in a procession starting from Philip Road

carnival week was a huge success and succeeded in raising £1,000 towards the playing field fund. Subsequent carnivals were held well into the 1950s to help raise money for the playing fields, which in due course were built as planned.

At a council meeting early in 1950, it was reported by the Borough Lands and Town Planning Committee that the ancient Market Cross was giving cause for concern, having deteriorated badly in the last two years. It was suggested that the only remedy was to take it down and rebuild it again in the same place. The cross had stood in this area for centuries, although its original position had been nearer to the church wall. Early in the eighteenth century the local gentry had found that it prevented them from getting their carriages near to the church gate, so the cross was taken down and rebuilt on its present site. The cross was often used as a platform by the town crier, and on other occasions it was used by the mayor to read out royal proclamations. Countless generations of weary travellers used the steps as seats, causing wear and tear on the stones. Unfortunately the majority of councillors decided that the cost of refurbishment, estimated at £80, could not be justified. One councillor

A proclamation is made by the mayor from the Market Cross

voiced a fear that if the work was put in hand the costs might rise and the town could end up with a supplementary rate of 6d.

Wilton resumed its historic connections with royalty later in the year, when Princess Margaret spent a weekend as the guest of the Earl and Countess of Pembroke at Wilton House. She arrived after attending an RAF display at Farnborough with the king and queen. Although this was a private visit, the princess did make one public appearance when she attended Sunday morning matins at the parish church. On entering, she was presented to an eighteen-year-old girl, who was paralysed and had been confined to a wheelchair for the last four years. After the service the princess was driven back to Wilton House through streets lined with cheering and waving onlookers.

This royal visit, like many others in the past, forged another link in a long chain stretching back to ancient times, when Wilton could justify its claim to be a royal town.

Acknowledgements

I would like to thank the following individuals and organizations for their help and assistance during the preparation of this publication: Mrs Marcia Holly, Mrs Pat Brown, Revd Dr John Gosling, Mr N. Crook, and, from the *Salisbury Journal*, the Editor, David Eidlestein and the News Editor, David Vallis.

Index